IT DEPENDS

Employee Relations Case Studies for Human Resources Professionals and Students

Angela Champ

Tellwell Talent
www.tellwell.ca

ISBN
978-1-77370-071-7 (Hardcover)
978-1-77370-070-0 (Paperback)
978-1-77370-072-4 (eBook)

TABLE OF CONTENTS

INTRODUCTION

The classic answer to just about every Human Resources issue is "it depends," and this collection of case studies demonstrates exactly why.

There is no one correct answer to the case studies in this book; however, there is usually one that is more correct than others. Employee relations are complex and nuanced, and the specific circumstances of a situation can change the outcome even when they appear identical to another situation; this illustrates why we must take a contextual approach when dealing with employee relations, including:

- The misconduct or incident in question;
- The length of the employment relationship;
- The nature of the employee's position and duties, and whether there is an extra burden, accountability or fiduciary duty on that employee;
- Any prior discipline;
- The employee's explanation for the misconduct or incident.

This book is intended for Human Resources students or any professional looking to increase their employee relations skills. The case studies in this collection are a composite of situations that you could realistically face in many non-unionized organizations. (For the purposes of this book, unionized case studies are not included as the outcome is often less "it depends" and more "What does the collective agreement say?" While legislation and common law do apply in unionized environments, the process for discipline, up to and including termination, is often spelled out in collective agreements.) While representative of real cases, any resemblance to organizations or persons, living or dead, is purely coincidental.

Use these case studies for discussion and to learn how to get to the best outcome possible. When reviewing these scenarios, research applicable legislation in your jurisdiction and in other provinces, states or countries, to see how the law changes across territories. For example, at the time of publishing this book, twenty-nine states in the United States of America have laws that legalize medical marijuana use while eight states have laws that legalize marijuana for recreational use; Canada is poised to enact similar legislation in 2018, and some other countries, such as Italy, have decriminalized the possession of small amounts of marijuana. This can greatly affect the outcome of the discussion and decisions in *Case Study 9 – The Drug Dilemma*, depending on which country or which state or province you are in.

As well, when reviewing these cases, look up case law to learn how precedence is applied and how common law (or Civil Code in Quebec) changes over time. The discussion questions are deliberately vague so that they can be applied to any jurisdiction, whether in Canada, the United States, or elsewhere in the world.

The minor changes in the various scenarios within each case study are meant to illustrate how small details can affect the outcome of any situation, which is why the classic answer to just about every Human Resources issue is, "it depends."

CASE STUDY 1

THE TARDY EMPLOYEE

SCENARIO 1

Ben is a twenty-four-year-old employee at The Prince Group, a large engineering firm that specializes in civil engineering projects, such as roads, bridges and infrastructure. Ben has been with the company for eight months; prior to this, he worked as a retail sales clerk for a men's store, but joined The Prince Group because he wanted to have better career opportunities. He works in a team of six from 8:00 a.m. to 4:00 p.m. as an Accounts Receivable Representative, and his work includes calling customers regarding outstanding invoices, processing payments, and issuing invoices. While he is not a star at work, he is considered a steady employee who makes few errors.

Ben has an easygoing and pleasant personality. In general, his coworkers like him, and he occasionally goes out for drinks after work with a group of guys from his office. He also just joined the company hockey team. However, Ben has come to work late four times in the past two weeks and his coworkers are starting to notice. Aside from this, there have been no performance or absenteeism issues.

When his manager, Jeff, spoke with Ben about his lateness, Ben replied, "Well, I guess I'm just not a morning person." Jeff mentioned this to you, his Human Resources representative, in passing during a conversation you were having about other staffing issues on the team.

DISCUSSION QUESTIONS

1. How would you approach this situation?

2. What advice would you give to Jeff?

3. What questions would you ask Jeff or Ben?

4. What are the contextual circumstances that have to be considered in this scenario that might have an effect on the outcome?

5. Would you recommend disciplinary action for Ben? Why or why not? If yes, what sort of discipline would you recommend?

6. Would your approach and advice differ if this was a single event versus a repeated event? How would it differ?

SCENARIO 2

Ben is a twenty-four-year-old employee at The Prince Group, a large engineering firm that specializes in civil engineering projects, such as roads, bridges and infrastructure. He has been with the company for eight months; prior to this, he worked as a retail sales clerk for a men's store, but joined The Prince Group because he wanted to have better career opportunities. He works in a team of six from 8:00 a.m. to 4:00 p.m. as an Accounts Receivable Representative, and his work includes calling customers regarding outstanding invoices, processing payments, and issuing invoices. While he is not a star at work, he is considered a steady employee who makes few errors.

Ben has an easygoing and pleasant personality. In general, his coworkers like him, and he occasionally goes out for drinks after work with a group of guys from his office. He also just joined the company hockey team. However, Ben has come to work late four times in the past two weeks and his coworkers are starting to notice. Ben has also called in sick five times in the past eight months. The company has a sick leave policy that allows for five sick days with pay every year, so Ben's sick leave has not been addressed.

When his manager, Jeff, spoke with Ben about his recent lateness, Ben replied, "Well, I guess I'm just not a morning person." When you, the Human Resources representative, spoke with Ben about this, Ben mentioned that the bus schedule had changed recently and he could not get to the office before 8:20 a.m. because of his reliance on transit.

DISCUSSION QUESTIONS

1. Do Ben's five sick days factor into the approach you would take in this case?

2. What are the other contextual circumstances that have to be considered in this scenario that might have an effect on the outcome?

3. What advice would you give to Jeff to resolve this issue now that you know that Ben's bus does not get him to the office until 8:20? Does Ben's reliance on public transport change your advice from Scenario 1?

4. Would you recommend disciplinary action for Ben? Why or why not? If yes, what would be appropriate in this case?

5. Would your approach and advice differ if this was a single event versus a repeated event? How would it differ?

SCENARIO 3

Ben is a forty-eight-year-old employee at The Prince Group, a large engineering firm that specializes in civil engineering projects, such as roads, bridges and infrastructure. He has been with the company for eight months; prior to this, he worked as a retail sales clerk for a men's store, but joined The Prince Group because he wanted to have better career opportunities. He works in a team of six from 8:00 a.m. to 4:00 p.m. as an Accounts Receivable Representative, and his work includes calling customers regarding outstanding invoices, processing payments, and issuing invoices. Despite a four-week training period and frequent follow-up by his manager, Ben makes frequent mistakes which require redoing some work to correct the errors.

In general, his coworkers like him, and he occasionally goes out for drinks after work with a group of guys from his office. He also just joined the company hockey team. However, Ben has come to work late four times in the past two weeks and his coworkers are starting to notice. There have also been some rumblings from the team about having to correct Ben's mistakes or deal with irate customers resulting from Ben's errors.

When his manager, Jeff, spoke with Ben about his recent lateness, Ben replied, "Well, I guess I'm just not a morning person." Jeff has come to you, the Human Resources representative, to ask for advice on what to do with Ben.

DISCUSSION QUESTIONS

1. What are the issues here? What questions would you ask Jeff? What do you need to know about Ben and his situation?

2. Which behaviour in this situation is conduct and which is performance? How would you explain the difference to Jeff?

3. Would you address both issues together with Ben and Jeff, or focus on just one? If just one, which one, and why?

4. What course of action would you recommend to Jeff? Why?

5. Does Ben's age affect how you would approach this scenario compared with Scenarios 1 and 2? Why or why not?

6. Would your approach and advice differ if this was a single event versus a repeated event? How would it differ?

CASE STUDY 2

THE HARASSMENT

SCENARIO 1

Southern Lights Ltd. is committed to a respectful work environment and has recently implemented a diversity and respect in the workplace training program for all of its three thousand six hundred employees. At the end of one training session, Amir, a three-year employee, approached Susan, the diversity specialist, to speak to her about a concern he had about his workplace. After hearing his concern, Susan suggested that Amir meet with Human Resources to discuss the issue.

When Amir arrives for his meeting with you, the Human Resources Business Partner, he hands you a three-page typed statement, which outlines the ways that he feels he is being harassed and disrespected at work. Specifically, he complains that the team of four women he works with are purposely "showing off" their bare arms and armpits, which goes against his cultural beliefs and comfort level. With summer temperatures soaring at thirty degrees Celsius, the women have been wearing sundresses or sleeveless tops to work and Amir is offended by their "display of immodesty."

In his statement, Amir has included a definition of "harassment" that he took out of the *Respect in the Workplace* training material:

> "Harassment is the act of systematic and/or continued unwanted and annoying actions of one party or a group, including threats and demands. The purposes may vary, including racial prejudice, personal malice, or merely to gain pleasure from making someone fearful or anxious. Such activities may be the basis for a lawsuit if due to discrimination based on race or sex, and a systematic

pattern of harassment by an employee against another worker may subject the employer to a lawsuit for failure to protect the employee."

Amir insists that you discipline these women and he is asking for restitution for the upset the situation has caused. He is threatening to sue the company for "failure to protect the employee" from what he sees as systematic harassment if the situation is not addressed.

While you do not know Amir well, you have been working with Margo, the manager of this team, for a few weeks, coaching her on how to resolve conflict among team members. You have learned from Margo that three of the women on the team are friends outside of the office and have worked together for over ten years, that a fourth female team member has complained about the clique, and that Amir seems to be a misfit within the team. However, all five team members have a specialized skill set and generally perform their jobs well. Despite the dysfunctional team dynamic, each individual is considered good at their jobs.

DISCUSSION QUESTIONS

1. How would you approach this situation? What would you say to Amir?

2. Do you agree with Amir that he is being harassed? What resources would you access to research this?

3. Would you speak with the women on his team? Why or why not? If yes, what would you say to them?

4. There are several issues within Margo's team. How would you advise Margo on how to address these conflicts within her team?

5. What are the contextual circumstances that have to be considered in this scenario that might have an effect on the outcome?

SCENARIO 2

Southern Lights Ltd. is committed to a respectful work environment and has recently implemented a diversity and respect in the workplace training program for all of its three thousand six hundred employees. At the end of one training session, Sarah, a three-year employee, approached Susan, the diversity specialist, to speak to her about a concern she had about her workplace. After hearing her concern, Susan suggested that Sarah meet with Human Resources to discuss the issue.

When Sarah arrives for her meeting with you, the Human Resources Business Partner, she hands you a three-page typed statement which outlines the ways that she feels she is being harassed and disrespected at work. Specifically, she complains that the four men she works with frequently make blonde jokes, seemingly aimed at her, and comment on her clothing, saying things like, "That skirt makes your legs look long," or "That dress really shows off your figure."

In her statement, Sarah has included a definition of "harassment" that she took out of the *Respect in the Workplace* training material:

> "Harassment is the act of systematic and/or continued unwanted and annoying actions of one party or a group, including threats and demands. The purposes may vary, including racial prejudice, personal malice, or merely to gain pleasure from making someone fearful or anxious. Such activities may be the basis for a lawsuit if due to discrimination based on race or sex, and a systematic pattern of harassment by an employee against another worker may subject the employer to a lawsuit for failure to protect the employee."

Sarah insists that you discipline these men and she is asking for restitution for the upset the situation has caused. At one point, the conversation with Sarah becomes emotionally charged and she threatens to sue the company for "failure to protect the employee" from what she sees as systematic harassment if the situation is not addressed.

You know that Sarah is a good employee and she has not complained before about her colleagues. Five years prior, another employee, also female, had complained about one of the men on the team, Bob, about a similar situation. Your predecessor had spoken to Bob and there was a note on the file about the incident. No disciplinary action had been taken at the time, and the note itself does not state any follow up or consequences to Bob, other than to document the conversation. At the time, the Human Resources representative told Bob that he had to apologize to the employee and to promise not to do it again. When you look into this further, you see that Bob is considered a "high potential" employee and is on the promotion fast track.

DISCUSSION QUESTIONS

1. How would you approach this situation? What would you say to Sarah?

2. Do you agree with Sarah that she is facing harassment? What resources would you access to research this?

3. How is this scenario different than Scenario 1?

4. Would you speak with Bob and the others on this team? Why or why not? If yes, what would you say to them?

5. The manager on this team, Margo, was the same manager on the team when Bob was spoken to five years ago. Does Margo share any liability in this?

6. Because Bob is on the "high potential" list, he is being mentored by the COO of the company. Everyone believes that this makes Bob "untouchable" and unlikely to be disciplined in any way. How would you go about this in that case?

7. Research the legislation in your jurisdiction for sexual or other harassment in the workplace. What is the liability on the part of the organization should Sarah be able to prove that she is being harassed?

8. Should Bob be terminated? Why or why not?

9. What is needed to ensure that these situations do not occur in the workplace? What policies should be implemented?

10. Research effective harassment policies that you could use.

11. How do you have to communicate such policies in order to make them enforceable? What are the criteria required for effective policies?

CASE STUDY 3

THE MORTGAGE APPLICATION

SCENARIO 1

You are picking up your voicemail messages at the end of the day and listen to one that leaves you perplexed:

> "Hi, this is Maria from Prospect Bank. I'm calling you to clarify some details in the letter you provided to Julie Rogers for her mortgage application. Could you please call me at 555-1212 at your earliest opportunity? Thank you for your time."

You know Julie Rogers as one of the Marketing Coordinators in the office, but you have no recollection of providing a letter to her recently. As it is the end of the day, you decide to leave it for now and look into it in the morning.

The next day, you pull Julie's file and see that she has been with the company for just over three years. She is twenty-eight years old and had previously worked for one of your competitors, so came with industry experience. She started as a temporary employee and was hired permanently six months into her role to replace someone who had resigned. In her first performance review, she received three out of five, with five being the highest rating. In her second year, she received four out of five, and in this last most recent review, she received another three out of five rating. You do not see anything unusual in her file – no notes from her manager, no absenteeism, nothing of a disciplinary nature. However, you also do not see any letter for a mortgage application either.

Confused, you call Maria from Prospect Bank. During your conversation, she tells you that she is referencing a letter signed by you but that she has some questions in order to complete Julie's mortgage application. You ask Maria to e-mail you a copy of the letter, as you have no recollection of sending one. A few minutes later, you open the attachment in Maria's e-mail and see that the letter was printed on company letterhead and signed in your name, but the signature was forged.

DISCUSSION QUESTIONS

1. What steps would you take to investigate this situation?

2. In the three years that Julie has worked for the company, her work has been satisfactory and there have been no problems. Does this factor into your approach in this situation? Why or why not?

3. What are the other contextual circumstances that have to be considered in this scenario that might have an effect on the outcome?

During the course of your investigation, you become convinced that Julie wrote the letter and forged your signature herself, although she denies doing so. You do not believe that another employee would have done this, and if another employee had, that person would have been an accomplice to this infraction. However, Julie insists that she has no idea how this letter was written or sent to Prospect Bank. Maria told you that Julie had sent the letter through an e-mail attachment from Julie's personal e-mail address a few days prior.

1. Based on the facts listed above, do you believe that Julie's behaviour has irreparably harmed the employment relationship to the point where the employer can no longer trust her? Why or why not?

2. Would you terminate Julie? Why or why not? If yes, would you terminate "with cause" or "without cause"?

3. Research recent case law in "just cause" terminations. What is the primary criteria for "just cause" terminations? Does this case apply?

4. What other alternatives are there to "just cause" termination?

5. Would your approach be different if Julie was fifty-five years old with thirty years of service with the company, rather than twenty-eight years old with three years of service? Why or why not?

6. If you decided to terminate "without cause," outline the severance package you would give to twenty-eight-year-old Julie. What would the package be for fifty-five-year-old Julie? Is it the same? Why or why not? What are the factors to take into account when determining appropriate severance pay?

SCENARIO 2

You are picking up your voicemail messages at the end of the day and listen to one that leaves you perplexed:

> "Hi, this is Maria from Prospect Bank. I'm calling you to clarify some details in the letter you provided to Julie Rogers for her mortgage application. Could you please call me at 555-1212 at your earliest opportunity? Thank you for your time."

You know Julie Rogers as one of the Marketing Coordinators in the office, but you have no recollection of providing a letter to her recently. As it is the end of the day, you decide to leave it for now and look into it in the morning.

The next day, you pull Julie's file and see that she has been with the company for just over three years. She is twenty-eight years old and had previously worked for one of your competitors, so came with industry experience. She started as a temporary employee and was hired permanently six months into her role to replace someone who had resigned. In her first performance review, she received three out of five, with five being the highest rating. In her second year, she received four out of five, and in this last recent review, she received another three out of five rating. You do not see anything unusual in her file – no notes from her manager, no absenteeism, nothing of a disciplinary nature. However, you also do not see any letter for a mortgage application either.

Confused, you call Maria from Prospect Bank. During your conversation, she tells you that she is referencing a letter signed by you but that she has some questions in order to complete Julie's mortgage application. You ask Maria to e-mail you a copy of the letter, as you have no recollection of sending one. A few minutes later, you open the attachment in Maria's e-mail and see that the letter was printed on company letterhead and signed in your name, but the signature was forged.

During the course of your investigation, you learn that Julie has a roommate, Tracy Jenkins, who is also an employee of your company. Tracy works in the accounting department and has been with the company less than one year. Julie insists that she did not forge a letter; instead, she tells you that Tracy had offered to obtain the mortgage letter from Human Resources on her behalf. Julie seems confused about your claim that your signature was forged.

DISCUSSION QUESTIONS

1. How would your approach change in Scenario 2 versus Scenario 1? What steps would you take?

2. If you believe that Julie accepted the letter from Tracy as legitimate, would it change the outcome for Julie? How?

3. If Tracy admits to forging the letter and passing it along to Julie, what outcome would you recommend for Tracy? Would this be a "with cause" or "without cause" termination? Explain your rationale for either decision.

CASE STUDY 4

THE BIG BENEFIT

SCENARIO 1

Carole Littleton is a receptionist at Horowitz Accounting. She has worked in the role for four years and was hired as a referral from her niece, Judy, who has worked for the company for thirteen years as a Certified General Accountant.

Carole suffered an accident the previous year, when she fell down the stairs in her home. She had injured her back and was frequently in pain. At fifty-nine years old, the doctor told Carole that her back pain may never improve. To accommodate her situation, the company provided Carole with a sit-stand desk to help alleviate the pain and to make the working conditions more tolerable.

However, today you received an e-mail from your company's benefits provider saying that they were investigating false claims submitted by Carole over the course of the last year. From the e-mail, you learn that Carole submitted seven claims for physiotherapy, but that the dates did not correspond with the physiotherapist's records. In total, $840 in claims was in question. The benefits provider advised you that they will be pursuing a fraud investigation.

Because trust and integrity are vital to your company's reputation, Horowitz Accounting has a zero-tolerance policy for fraud or dishonesty from its employees. During your investigation, Carole admits to submitting false claims for physiotherapy but tells you that she did it because she needed the money; her husband lost his job several months prior and their debts were piling up. Carole felt desperate and did not think that anyone would find out. During the interview, Carole broke down in tears and begged you not to fire her, as she needs this job and losing it would put her and her husband into an even direr situation. She believes that her age and her injury will prevent her from finding other work. She also tells you that her husband is abusive and, if she lost her job, he would likely hurt her.

DISCUSSION QUESTIONS

1. How would you approach this situation? What are the contextual circumstances that have to be considered in this scenario that might have an effect on the outcome?

2. Would you show Carole any leniency for admitting that she submitted false claims?

3. Does the total dollar amount of the submitted claims factor into your decision at all? Why or why not?

4. Would you terminate Carole? If so, would you terminate her "with cause" or "without cause"? Explain your rationale for choosing either approach.

5. Does the fact that Carole's niece works for Horowitz Accounting factor into your decision at all? Why or why not?

6. Do Carole's personal circumstances factor into your decision at all? Why or why not?

7. Would you insist that Carole repay the $840? What legal recourse would you have for recovering the $840 from Carole?

8. What resources would you provide to Carole, if any?

SCENARIO 2

Carole Littleton is a receptionist at Horowitz Accounting. She has worked in the role for four years and was hired as a referral from her niece, Judy, who has worked for the company for thirteen years as a Certified General Accountant.

Carole suffered an accident the previous year, when she fell down the stairs in her home. She had injured her back and was frequently in pain. At fifty-nine years old, the doctor told Carole that her back pain may never improve. To accommodate her situation, the company provided Carole with a sit-stand desk to help alleviate the pain and to make the working conditions more tolerable.

However, today you received an e-mail from your company's benefits provider saying that they were investigating false claims submitted by Carole over the course of the last year. From the e-mail, you learn that Carole submitted seven claims for physiotherapy, but that the dates did not correspond with the physiotherapist's records. In total, $630 in claims was in question, and copies of the claims submissions were included in the e-mail. The benefits provider advised you that they will be pursuing a fraud investigation.

Because trust and integrity are vital to your company's reputation, Horowitz Accounting has a zero-tolerance policy for fraud or dishonesty from its employees, and you believe you will need to terminate Carole's employment immediately. However, during your investigation, Carole denies submitting any physiotherapy claims to the benefits provider in the past year. She states that she has been taking massage therapy to alleviate her back pain. When you show Carole the claims submissions from the e-mail, Carole stresses that the handwriting and signatures are not hers. She speculates that her husband, Arnold, was submitting false claims in her name.

DISCUSSION QUESTIONS

1. How would you approach this situation? What are the contextual circumstances that have to be considered in this scenario that might have an effect on the outcome?

2. If the investigation bears out that Arnold submitted the false claims without Carole's knowledge, would you terminate Carole? Why or why not?

3. Would you insist that Carole repay the $630 in claims? Would you be able to legally recover the $630 from Carole?

CASE STUDY 5

THE REFERENCE

SCENARIO 1

You receive a phone call from a recruiter from Frinkle Winkle Candy Company. They are looking to hire Carole Littleton as a receptionist and have called you for a reference as her previous employer.

You remember that Carole used to work as a receptionist for your company but you terminated her last year. (See *Case Study 4, Scenario 1*).

DISCUSSION QUESTIONS

1. Would you provide a reference for Carole (based on information from *Case Study 4, Scenario 1*)? Why or why not?

2. If you decide to provide a reference for Carole, what would you say? Would you tell Frinkle Winkle Candy Company the circumstances of Carole's departure?

3. If you did not want to provide a reference for Carole, what would you say to the recruiter?

4. Does privacy legislation in your jurisdiction affect what you can say about Carole to Frinkle Winkle Candy Company? Research which privacy legislation might apply in this case.

SCENARIO 2

You receive a phone call from a recruiter from Frinkle Winkle Candy Company. They are looking to hire Carole Littleton as a receptionist and have called you for a reference as her previous employer. By coincidence, the recruiter is a good friend of yours. After you terminated Carole last year (see *Case Study 4, Scenario 1*), you had talked about the situation with a small group of good friends over wine, including this recruiter. While you did not mention Carole's name at the time, you were all sharing "war stories" about your respective workplaces and the kinds of situations you deal with at work.

DISCUSSION QUESTIONS

1. Would you provide a reference for Carole (based on information from *Case Study 4, Scenario 1*)? Why or why not?

2. Since the recruiter is a friend of yours, would you remind her of the story you shared during your night out and let her know you were referring to Carole?

3. If you did not want to provide a reference for Carole, what would you say to the recruiter? What if your friend pressed you on this?

4. Does privacy legislation in your jurisdiction affect what you can say about Carole to your friend? Research which privacy legislation might apply in this case.

CASE STUDY 6

THE CONNECTIONS

SCENARIO 1

Your company is in the final stages of recruiting a new salesperson. The final candidate, Frank Neusome, seems to have it all: good sales experience, demonstrated results, strong contacts in the business, and a personality that will fit in with your organizational culture. The assessment he completed shows that he is a strong candidate for the role.

As a last step, you want to call Frank's references. He has given you three names, all of whom work with Frank's former employer, not his current one. The hiring manager, Joe, mentions that he knows a couple of people who work at Frank's current employer and is going to call them to "get the goods" on Frank.

DISCUSSION QUESTIONS

1. What are the concerns about Joe phoning his connections at Frank's current employer?

2. What are the potential consequences of Joe calling Frank's colleagues to ask about him?

3. Are there any privacy or consent laws that your organization needs to follow when recruiting? Do these laws apply to Frank's situation?

4. What would you advise Joe to do in this situation?

SCENARIO 2

Your company is in the final stages of recruiting a new salesperson. The final candidate, Frank Neusome, seems to have it all: good sales experience, demonstrated results, strong contacts in the business, and a personality that will fit in with your organizational culture. The assessment he completed shows that he is a strong candidate for the role.

You are preparing the letter of offer when your phone rings. It is Frank, and he is absolutely livid. He is yelling into the phone, and at first you are having trouble following what he is saying. Finally, you piece together that Frank is angry because his current employer, a competitor of yours, found out about Frank's candidacy and terminated his employment effective that afternoon. According to Frank, someone from your company called one of his colleagues to ask about him, and that colleague told Frank's boss.

After calming Frank down and promising to get back to him as soon as possible, you meet with Joe, the hiring manager, to let him know about the call. Joe admits that he called Frank's colleague, who is a friend. Joe says, "I don't see what the big deal is. We were going to hire Frank anyway."

DISCUSSION QUESTIONS

1. What are the concerns about Joe phoning his friend at Frank's current employer?

2. What are the potential consequences of Joe calling Frank's colleagues to ask about him?

3. Are there any privacy or consent laws that your organization needs to follow when recruiting? Do these laws apply to Frank's situation?

4. What would you advise Joe to do in this situation?

5. What would you do with Frank? Is there any restitution?

6. What if your company decided at the last minute not to make an offer to Frank? Would there be any recourse for him? Would there be any liability on the part of your organization?

CASE STUDY 7

THE ACCOMMODATION

SCENARIO 1

Sangheeta works as an Office Administrator at Beacon Enterprises, a company of eight hundred employees, and supervises a team of five. She has worked for the organization for over twelve years, starting in an entry level role and promoting into management one step at a time. Her performance reviews have always been four or five out of five, with five being the best rating. Her team likes her and Sangheeta is friendly with everyone in the company.

In the past year, Sangheeta has had some health issues, stemming from a motor vehicle accident in which she injured her back, her right leg, and her right shoulder. She is still undergoing treatment for her physical injuries and is frequently tired at the end of the day. She finds it difficult to sit at her desk and she has trouble navigating the stairs of the two-storey office space. Unfortunately, her physical injuries have also brought on depression and anxiety, and Sangheeta has missed several weeks of work on and off since the accident as a result of both the physical injuries and the mental stress.

Sangheeta's boss, Alexa, is starting to become frustrated with Sangheeta's frequent absences. She called in sick today, leaving the team scrambling to cover for a presentation that Sangheeta was supposed to make to the COO. "I know she is a good employee," said Alexa, "but we're running a business here. She's been missing a lot of work lately and it's been falling in everyone else's lap to take care of her work. People are starting to get frustrated, and her team is now coming directly to me. I don't have time for this! Isn't there anything we can do?"

DISCUSSION QUESTIONS

1. How would you approach this situation? What are the options for Beacon Enterprises?

2. What conversations might you have with Sangheeta?

3. How would you coach Alexa in this matter?

4. How would you address the team?

5. Research the legislation available in your jurisdiction on disabilities and duty to accommodate. What are the conditions under which an employer has a duty to accommodate, and what exceptions are there?

6. How does the legislation on disabilities and duty to accommodate in your jurisdiction differ from legislation in other jurisdictions? How is it the same?

SCENARIO 2

Sangheeta works as an Office Administrator at Beacon Enterprises, a company of eight hundred employees, and supervises a team of five. She has worked for the organization for over twelve years, starting in an entry level role and promoting into management one step at a time. Her performance reviews have always been average. Sangheeta is not a star but is considered a steady employee with good knowledge of the organization.

In the past year, Sangheeta has had some health issues, stemming from a motor vehicle accident in which she injured her back, her right leg, and her right shoulder. She is still undergoing treatment for her physical injuries and is frequently tired at the end of the day. She finds it difficult to sit at her desk and she has trouble navigating the stairs of the two-storey office space. Unfortunately, her physical injuries have also brought on depression and anxiety, and Sangheeta has missed several weeks of work on and off since the accident as a result of both the physical injuries and the mental stress.

Sangheeta's team has been complaining to Alexa, Sangheeta's boss, about her frequent absences and that Sangheeta has been rude to various team members, criticizing them during team meetings and focusing on small errors. Alexa has come to you for advice on how to deal with the situation. "I know she is a long-term employee," said Alexa, "but we're running a business here. She's been missing a lot of work lately and it's been falling in everyone else's lap to take care of her work. People are starting to get frustrated, and her team is now coming directly to me. I don't have time for this! Isn't there anything we can do?"

DISCUSSION QUESTIONS

1. How would you approach this situation? What are the options for Beacon Enterprises?

2. What conversations might you have with Sangheeta?

3. Is there any discipline merited in this case? Why or why not?

4. How would you coach Alexa in this matter?

5. How would you address the team?

6. Research the legislation available in your jurisdiction on disabilities and duty to accommodate. What are the conditions under which an employer has a duty to accommodate, and what exceptions are there?

7. How does the legislation on disabilities and duty to accommodate in your jurisdiction differ from legislation in other jurisdictions? How is it the same?

SCENARIO 3

Sangheeta works as an Office Administrator at Beacon Enterprises, a company of eight hundred employee, and supervises a team of five. She has worked for the organization for over twelve years, starting in an entry level role and promoting into management one step at a time. Her performance reviews have always been average. Sangheeta is not a star but is considered a steady employee with good knowledge of the organization.

In the past year, Sangheeta has had some health issues, stemming from a motor vehicle accident a year prior. Her doctor has cleared her to return to work and your disability provider has advised that they do not support any disability leave of absence or further accommodation. Still, Sangheeta says that she finds it difficult to sit at her desk and she has trouble navigating the stairs of the two-storey office space. Sangheeta has also told her boss, Alexa, that she suffers from depression and anxiety, and Sangheeta has missed several weeks of work on and off since the accident as a result of both the physical injuries and the mental stress.

Sangheeta's team has been complaining to Alexa about her frequent absences and that Sangheeta has been rude to various team members, criticizing them during team meetings and focusing on small errors. Alexa has come to you for advice on how to deal with the situation. "I know she is a long-term employee," said Alexa, "but we're running a business here. She's been missing a lot of work lately and it's been falling in everyone else's lap to take care of her work. People are starting to get frustrated, and her team is now coming directly to me. I don't have time for this! Isn't there anything we can do?"

DISCUSSION QUESTIONS

1. How would you approach this situation? What are the options for Beacon Enterprises?

2. What conversations might you have with Sangheeta?

3. Is there any discipline merited in this case? Why or why not?

4. How would you coach Alexa in this matter?

5. How would you address the team?

6. Research the legislation available in your jurisdiction on disabilities and duty to accommodate. What are the conditions under which an employer has a duty to accommodate, and what exceptions are there?

7. Should Beacon Enterprises offer accommodation for Sangheeta? Why or why not? If yes, what sort of accommodation?

8. How does the legislation on disabilities and duty to accommodate in your jurisdiction differ from legislation in other jurisdictions? How is it the same?

CASE STUDY 8

THE PATRON

SCENARIO 1

Christina Papproupa, a manager in your company, Aztec Ventures, has asked to speak to you about a phone call she received earlier that morning. She tells you that the owner of a local bar that is popular with employees in your company had called to complain about one of Aztec's employees.

"The owner, Lisa, claims that one of our employees was abusive and rude to the wait staff at the bar last night and she wants to file a complaint," Christina tells you. "The owner identified the employee from the Aztec Ventures jacket he was wearing, and she got his name from the credit card he used to pay the bill.

"According to Lisa, the employee, Don White, apparently started yelling at the servers, calling them 'hos' because it was taking a long time to get his drinks. Don's companions were laughing and egging him on." Christina said that Lisa is threatening to go to the media with this, and plans to ban Aztec Ventures employees from the bar.

You learn that this incident occurred after work hours, at around 8:30 p.m., and it is not clear if Don's companions were also Aztec Venture employees.

DISCUSSION QUESTIONS

1. How would you approach this situation?

2. Does the organization have a right to direct an employee's behaviour after work hours, when they are on their own time?

3. Research recent case law to see what the courts say about a company's right to monitor employee actions outside of the office.

4. Would you meet with Don? What would you ask or tell him?

5. Would you recommend any disciplinary action against Don? Why or why not? If yes, what would that be?

6. Would you follow up with Lisa, the bar owner? What would you say?

SCENARIO 2

Christina Papproupa, a manager in your company, Aztec Ventures, has asked to speak to you about a phone call she received a few moments ago. She tells you that the owner of a local restaurant that is popular with employees in your company had called to complain about one of Aztec's employees.

"The owner, Lisa, claims that one of our employees was abusive and rude to the wait staff at lunch today and she wants to file a complaint," Christina tells you. "The owner identified the employee from the Aztec Ventures jacket he was wearing, and she got his name from the credit card he used to pay the bill.

"According to Lisa, the employee, Don White, apparently was unhappy with his meal and started yelling at the server." Christina said that Lisa is threatening to go to the media with this, and plans to ban Aztec Ventures employees from the restaurant.

Aztec Ventures allows one hour off for lunch, unpaid, and most employees go out to eat rather than use the office lunchroom.

DISCUSSION QUESTIONS

1. How would you approach this situation?

2. Does the organization have a right to direct an employee's behaviour during their unpaid time?

3. Research recent case law to see what the courts say about a company's right to monitor employee actions outside of the office.

4. Would you meet with Don? What would you ask or tell him?

5. Would you recommend any disciplinary action against Don? Why or why not? If yes, what would that be?

6. Would you follow up with Lisa, the restaurant owner? Why or why not? If yes, what would you say?

CASE STUDY 9

THE DRUG DILEMMA

SCENARIO 1

It is 9:30 p.m. on a Thursday evening and you are at home watching a movie on TV. Your cell phone rings and it is the district manager of your region, Kioko. She is phoning to tell you that one of your company's delivery drivers, Ryan, was in a motor vehicle accident while working. Ryan does not appear to be injured; however, when the police arrived at the accident scene, they found a bag of marijuana in the console of the vehicle, which Ryan admitted was his. The police have not charged Ryan with any offence. Kioko is at the accident scene with Ryan and is asking for advice on what to do.

Your company has a strict drugs and alcohol policy. All of your company's delivery drivers undergo extensive safety training once a year, and the drugs and alcohol policy is included in that training. In addition to random drug testing for all drivers, the company policy states that every driver must undergo a mandatory drug and alcohol test immediately following any accident, regardless of fault.

Ryan is a good driver and a good employee. In the six years that he has worked for your company, he has never had an accident or disciplinary incident.

DISCUSSION QUESTIONS

1. What is the first thing you would do in this scenario?

2. What sort of investigation would you conduct? What questions would you ask Ryan?

3. Research drug and alcohol legislation in your jurisdiction. Is random testing permitted?

4. Research effective drug and alcohol policies that would apply in your jurisdiction. What elements do they have that make them effective?

5. Assume you work in a jurisdiction where marijuana is legalized. Does this affect how you investigate this situation?

6. What are the contextual circumstances that have to be considered in this scenario that might have an effect on the outcome?

7. Would you terminate Ryan in this situation? Why or why not?

SCENARIO 2

It is 9:30 p.m. on a Thursday evening and you are at home watching a movie on TV. Your cell phone rings and it is the district manager of your region, Kioko. She is phoning to tell you that one of your company's delivery drivers, Ryan, was in a motor vehicle accident while working. Ryan does not appear to be injured; however, when the police arrived at the accident scene, they found a bag of marijuana in the console of the vehicle, which Ryan admitted was his. The police have charged Ryan with driving while impaired and Kioko is asking for advice on what to do.

Your company has a strict drugs and alcohol policy. All of your company's delivery drivers undergo extensive safety training once a year, and the drugs and alcohol policy is included in that training. In addition to random drug testing for all drivers, the company policy states that every driver must undergo a mandatory drug and alcohol test immediately following any accident, regardless of fault.

In this case, it is not possible to send Ryan for a mandatory drug or alcohol test as he is in jail.

Ryan is a good driver and a good employee. In the six years that he has worked for your company, he has never had an accident or disciplinary incident.

DISCUSSION QUESTIONS

1. How would you investigate this scenario? What are the contextual circumstances that have to be considered in this scenario that might have an effect on the outcome?

2. Kioko wants to terminate Ryan for driving while impaired. Under what circumstances, if any, can you terminate Ryan? Would it be "just cause" or "without just cause"?

3. Research "just cause" terminations. What criteria must be in place for this to be a "just cause" termination in your jurisdiction?

SCENARIO 3

It is 9:30 p.m. on a Thursday evening and you are at home watching a movie on TV. Your cell phone rings and it is the district manager of your region, Kioko. She is phoning to tell you that one of your company's delivery drivers, Ryan, was in a motor vehicle accident while working. Ryan does not appear to be injured; however, when the police arrived at the accident scene, they found a bag of marijuana in the console of the vehicle. Ryan has admitted that the marijuana is his and has told the police and Kioko that he has a medical certificate, which permits him to have and use it for his multiple sclerosis (MS) symptoms, which can be very debilitating.

Your company has a strict drugs and alcohol policy. All of your company's delivery drivers undergo extensive safety training once a year, and the drugs and alcohol policy is included in that training. In addition to random drug testing for all drivers, the company policy states that every driver must undergo a mandatory drug and alcohol test immediately following any accident, regardless of fault.

Ryan is a good driver and a good employee. In the six years he has worked for your company, he has never had an accident or disciplinary incident. Up until this moment, you were unaware that Ryan suffered from MS or that he had a medical certificate to use marijuana for his symptoms.

DISCUSSION QUESTIONS

1. How would you investigate this scenario?

2. What does the legislation in your jurisdiction say about the possession and use of medical marijuana? What are an employee's responsibilities when he/she is using medical marijuana? What are the employer's responsibilities?

3. Is an accommodation for Ryan appropriate in this situation? Why or why not?

4. Is there any discipline necessary in this situation? Why or why not? If yes, what sort of discipline is appropriate? Would you terminate Ryan's employment?

CASE STUDY 10

THE INTOXICATED EMPLOYEE

SCENARIO 1

Sasha Loren is a Care Assistant and Companion for Home Hugs, an organization that provides in-home care and meal services for elderly people who have difficulties managing on their own. She joined Home Hugs in 2009, having previously worked as a Nurse Practitioner at a retirement centre. In her role, Sasha currently rotates between three clients, offering services ranging from dispensing medicine in pill and injection form, to bathing clients, to cooking meals, and even doing some light housekeeping. Because of her long tenure, Sasha is considered a senior employee and often mentors new hires.

Today, Sasha's manager received a call from the daughter of one of the clients. The daughter claimed that Sasha had arrived late at her mother's house for her shift, and that she appeared to be drunk. The client's daughter was angry and threatened to contact the ministry responsible for regulating companies such as Home Hugs to lodge a formal complaint. You have asked for a meeting with Sasha's manager, Syed, to discuss the situation and next steps.

During the meeting, you learn that the client's daughter could smell alcohol on Sasha's breath and became concerned. The daughter confronted Sasha and asked her to leave the client's house and not return. Syed tells you that there have been similar situations in the past. In each of these situations, Syed met with Sasha to discuss them with her, and a letter had been placed in her file. When you look through the employee file, you see disciplinary letters dated March 2010, June 2012 and February 2015. Scanning the letter from March 2010, you see that it referenced an incident where Sasha showed up late with a slurred voice, glazed eyes, and breath that smelled of alcohol. You notice the last paragraph of the letter, which states,

> "This letter will remain on your file for a period of two (2) years, at which point it will be purged, unless another such incident occurs within that two (2) year period."

This clause is written in all three letters on file.

Syed tells you that the first incident occurred during Sasha's divorce, which was described as "nasty and ugly." Sasha had not coped well with the divorce and admitted to using alcohol as a crutch. After the second incident in June 2012, Sasha was suspended from work for three days and was compelled to attend a mandatory counselling session through their employee assistance program.

A week ago, Sasha told Syed that she had been seeing a counsellor who recommended taking some time off work, but Syed denied the request because they were short-staffed.

Syed is frustrated by Sasha's behaviour, saying that it would cause a reputational risk with the clients and with the regulatory body which licences the organization. He wants to terminate Sasha with cause and is seeking your advice.

DISCUSSION QUESTIONS

1. Are Sasha's actions culpable or non-culpable? Why do you believe this?

2. The letters of March 2010, June 2012 and February 2015, each have a "sunset clause," which indicates that the letters would be purged in two years from the date of letter unless there was a repeat incident. Should these letters have been purged?

3. If these letters should have been purged, can you rely on them to determine if "just cause" is merited in this case?

4. Syed seemed aware that Sasha had a history of drinking. Does the employer have a duty to accommodate even if the employee does not admit to any addiction? Research case law and legislation from your jurisdiction to learn what the law says in this regard.

5. Do you support Syed's decision to terminate Sasha's employment? Why or why not? If yes, would you terminate "just cause" or "without cause"?

SCENARIO 2

Sasha Loren is a Care Assistant and Companion for Home Hugs, an organization that provides in-home care and meal services for elderly people who have difficulties managing on their own. She joined Home Hugs in 2009, having previously worked as a Nurse Practitioner at a retirement centre. In her role, Sasha currently rotates between three clients, offering services ranging from dispensing medicine in pill and injection form, to bathing clients, to cooking meals, and even doing some light housekeeping. Because of her long tenure, Sasha is considered a senior employee and often mentors new hires.

Today, Sasha's manager received a call from the daughter of one of the clients. The daughter claimed that Sasha had arrived late at her mother's house for her shift, and that she appeared to be drunk. The client's daughter was angry and threatened to contact the ministry responsible for regulating companies such as Home Hugs to lodge a formal complaint. You have asked for a meeting with Sasha's manager, Syed, to discuss the situation and next steps.

During the meeting, you learn that the client's daughter could smell alcohol on Sasha's breath and became concerned. The daughter confronted Sasha and asked her to leave the client's house and not to return. Syed tells you that there have been similar situations in the past, though he could not remember the dates. In each of these situations, Syed met with Sasha to discuss them with her, but no letter or notes had been placed in her file.

Syed recalls that the first incident occurred around the time of Sasha's divorce several years ago, which was described as "nasty and ugly." Sasha

coped well with the divorce and admitted to using alcohol as a
.n.

A week ago, Sasha told Syed that she had been seeing a counsellor who recommended taking some time off work, but Syed denied the request because they were short-staffed.

Syed is frustrated by Sasha's behaviour, saying that it would cause a reputational risk with the clients and with the regulatory body which licences the organization. He wants to terminate Sasha with cause and is seeking your advice.

DISCUSSION QUESTIONS

1. Are Sasha's actions culpable or non-culpable? Why do you believe this?

2. There are no letters or other documentation on file regarding these incidents. Does this change your approach and advice to Syed from scenario 1? Why or why not?

3. Syed seemed aware that Sasha had a history of drinking. Does the employer have a duty to accommodate even if the employee does not admit to any addiction? Research case law and legislation from your jurisdiction to learn what the law says in this regard.

4. Do you support Syed's decision to terminate Sasha's employment? Why or why not? If yes, would you terminate "with cause" or "without cause"?

CASE STUDY 11

THE DRESS CODE

SCENARIO 1

You are a Human Resources Generalist for Pietro's Pizza, a chain of restaurants that is popular with young adults between the ages of eighteen and thirty-five. Two years ago, Pietro's Pizza was primarily a family restaurant, but over the past twenty-four months it had been reinvented to appeal to a younger crowd: the owners renovated the restaurants to include sports lounges, they introduced a happy hour menu from 4:00 to 6:00 p.m., and they started hiring energetic university students as servers, bartenders and hostesses. Around the same time, Pietro's management introduced a dress code: gone were the black pants and branded red button-down short sleeve shirts. Now, the male employees wear black pants and black button-down long-sleeved shirts (with the cuffs rolled up), while the female employees wear body conscious black tank tops with short black skirts and high heels. Overall, these changes have been very successful for the chain; sales were up 200% over the prior year, and there were often line ups for tables on Thursday, Friday and Saturday evenings.

However, these changes did not come without challenges. Some long-time staff had been terminated, regular customers complained about the lack of family-friendly food choices, and there had been a Facebook backlash against their hiring practices after a candidate was rejected for not "fitting the mold."

Today you received a phone call from one of the servers, Natasha, who said she does not feel comfortable wearing the black tank top, short skirt and high heels at work, and wanted to wear black pants and a button-down shirt like the male employees. She told you during your discussion that she did not want to lose her job because she relies on the income from her wages and tips to pay her university tuition, but also does not want to dress in a way that makes her feel immodest. She has been uncomfortable raising this with the restaurant manager for fear of repercussion and has asked you to intervene on her behalf.

DISCUSSION QUESTIONS

1. What does the law and human rights legislation in your jurisdiction say about dress in the workplace?

2. Can Natasha refuse to follow the dress code for female employees?

3. Can Natasha's employment be terminated if she does not want to follow this dress code? Should it be terminated?

4. What advice would you give to the management team of Pietro's Pizza chain of restaurants?

5. What recruitment or retention implications does this dress code create?

SCENARIO 2

You are a Human Resources Generalist for Southern Cross Consulting Group (SCCG), a management consulting firm that provides tax and consulting advice to some of the biggest companies in the country. The firm has been in business for fourteen years and annual revenues exceed six hundred million dollars. SCCG is owned by a group of five partners and is generally known in the industry as being very conservative and "blue chip." Associates, all MBA graduates, work long hours but are rewarded with high compensation and extra time off at the completion of project milestones.

Because of its clientele, SCCG has imposed a dress code for its employees: conservative suits in blue, grey or black for both men and women; no visible tattoos; no hair colour that is "not found naturally in nature"; no visible body piercings except for earrings on women; no beards on men; and neatly-coiffed hairstyles for both men and women.

Today, you and the office manager, Renaldo, are interviewing a candidate for an opening as a Senior Management Consultant. The candidate's resume is impeccable: graduated top of his class from a prestigious university; 5 years' experience with a well-known competitor; active in the community as a volunteer and board member of various charities; and demonstrated consulting success. However, in Renaldo's opinion there is a problem: the candidate has a diamond stud earring in his left ear, and a tattoo is visible on his wrist and knuckles of his right hand. Renaldo is concerned that the candidate's appearance will be a distraction for SCCG's clients, and may cause other SCCG associates to bend the rules of the dress code.

DISCUSSION QUESTIONS

1. What does the law and human rights codes in your jurisdiction say about dress in the workplace?

2. Can you and Renaldo decline to hire this candidate as a result of his visible body piercing and tattoo?

3. Can you ask employees to remove visible body piercings and to cover up tattoos while working?

4. What advice would you give to the management team of SCCG in this case?

CASE STUDY 12

THE DISCARDS

SCENARIO 1

Ming works as an Assistant Store Manager for Grewal Grocery, a supermarket located in an affluent section of town. He has worked there for six years, starting as a Stock Boy, then moving to Cashier before promoting into his current role. Ming knows many of the regular customers by name, and is well liked by the staff and by his manager, John.

The part of his job that Ming dislikes is throwing out expired food or day-old baked goods. Despite initiatives he has introduced to reduce the amount of food wastage, approximately one hundred pounds of expired food, such as yogurt, milk, cheese, bruised fruit and vegetables, and day-old muffins and donuts, is thrown out into the large metal garbage bin behind the store each day. "What a waste," he thinks. Ming knows that eating food that is past the expiry date is often not harmful. Manufacturers stamp a "best by" or "expiry" date on their products to maintain the best freshness and taste, but otherwise the food is edible for days or even weeks past the expiry date. However, customers are reluctant to buy food past the expiry date, or less-than-perfect fruit and vegetables.

One day, Ming hits upon the idea of donating some or all of the discarded food to a local homeless shelter. After the store closed, Ming returned with a ladder and some boxes, and he bagged and wrapped food, such as bread, out of the garbage bin and packed them into six boxes. He then drove the food to the homeless shelter and donated it. The volunteer staff at the shelter were extremely grateful for the donation. Ming did this after every shift for the next two weeks, feeling very glad that the food would not be wasted and would go to people in need.

By coincidence, his manager, John, was driving by one evening and noticed someone climbing into the store's garbage bin. He stopped his car and realized that it was Ming. John became very angry and confronted Ming, accusing him of theft. Ming explained what he had been doing with the food but John would not listen. He fired Ming on the spot and told him not to return to work the next day. John also told Ming that he would go to the police to bring criminal charges against Ming for his actions.

DISCUSSION QUESTIONS

1. Was John's reaction to the situation appropriate? Why or why not?

2. Should Ming's employment be terminated? Why or why not? If yes, "with cause" or "without cause"?

3. Should Ming have approached this situation a different way? How?

4. What advice would you give to John in this situation?

5. What needs to be in place for this situation not to reoccur?

SCENARIO 2

Ming works as an Assistant Store Manager for Grewal Grocery, a supermarket located in an affluent section of town. He has worked there for six years, starting as a Stock Boy, then moving to Cashier before promoting into his current role. Ming knows many of the regular customers by name, and is well liked by the staff and by his manager, John.

The part of his job that Ming dislikes is having to throw out expired food or day-old baked goods. Despite initiatives he has introduced to reduce the amount of food wastage, approximately one hundred pounds of expired food, such as yogurt, milk, cheese, bruised fruit and vegetables, and day-old muffins and donuts, is thrown out into the large metal garbage bin behind the store each day. "What a waste," he thinks. Ming knows that eating food that is past the expiry date is often not harmful. Manufacturers stamp a "best by" or "expiry" date on their products to maintain the best freshness and taste, but otherwise the food is edible for days or weeks past the expiry date. However, customers are reluctant to buy food past the expiry date, or less-than-perfect fruit and vegetables.

One day, Ming put aside some of the day-old bread, fruit, and vegetables, and brought them home to give to his neighbours, who are recent refugees and do not have much money. The family was very grateful for the food. Ming did this after every shift for the next two weeks, feeling very glad that the food would not be wasted.

Today, his manager, John, noticed Ming leaving the store with a box under his arm. He confronted Ming, asking what was in the box. Ming explained what he had been doing with the food but John became very angry and confronted Ming, accusing him of theft. He fired Ming on the spot and told him not to return to work the next day. John also told Ming that he would go to the police to bring criminal charges against Ming for his actions.

DISCUSSION QUESTIONS

1. Was John's reaction to the situation appropriate? Why or why not?

2. Should Ming's employment be terminated? Why or why not? If yes, "with cause" or "without cause"?

3. Should Ming have approached this situation a different way? How?

4. What advice would you give to John in this situation?

5. Is this situation different than Scenario 1? Why or why not?

6. What needs to be in place for this situation not to reoccur?

SCENARIO 3

Ming works as an Assistant Store Manager for Grewal Grocery, a supermarket located in an affluent section of town. He has worked there for six years, starting as a Stock Boy, then moving to Cashier before promoting into his current role. Ming knows many of the regular customers by name, and is well liked by the staff and by his manager, John.

The part of his job that Ming dislikes is having to throw out expired food or day-old baked goods. Despite initiatives he has introduced to reduce the amount of food wastage, approximately one hundred pounds of expired food, such as yogurt, milk, cheese, bruised fruit and vegetables, and day-old muffins and donuts, is thrown out into the large metal garbage bin behind the store each day. "What a waste," he thinks. Ming knows that eating food that is past the expiry date is often not harmful. Manufacturers stamp a "best by" or "expiry" date on their products to maintain the best freshness and taste, but otherwise the food is edible for days or weeks past the expiry date. However, customers are reluctant to buy food past the expiry date, or less-than-perfect fruit and vegetables.

One day, one of the employees, Clarence, asked Ming if he could take some of the discarded food and donate it to a homeless shelter. Ming agreed and, over the next two weeks, helped Clarence box up and donate several hundred pounds of expired but otherwise edible food. Both Ming and Clarence were very glad that the food would not be wasted.

Today, his manager, John, noticed Clarence and Ming boxing up food and asked what was going on. Ming explained what they had been doing with the food but John became very angry and confronted Ming, accusing both

Clarence and Ming of theft. He fired them on the spot and told them not to return to work the next day. John also told Ming that he would go to the police to bring criminal charges against him and Clarence for their actions.

DISCUSSION QUESTIONS

1. Was John's reaction to the situation appropriate? Why or why not?

2. Should Ming's employment be terminated? Why or why not? If yes, "with cause" or "without cause"?

3. Should Clarence's employment be terminated? Why or why not? If yes, "with cause" or "without cause"?

4. What advice would you give to John in this situation?

5. Is this situation different than Scenario 1 and 2? How?

CASE STUDY 13

THE TERMINATION

SCENARIO 1

Marcello has worked as a graphic designer in a small boutique ad agency for the past two years. There was always pressure to meet deadlines, and working with a creative, driven group was often stressful. Still, he loved his job, despite the many flare-ups in the office.

However, lately Marcello's boss, Cynthia, had been pretty hard on the team of eight. Their current client was unhappy with the ideas that the team had presented at their last meeting and they were in danger of losing the account. After a particularly heated pitch meeting, Cynthia stood up and yelled at Marcello, "Go! Get out! I'm sick of you and your stupid, boring ideas! You don't have a creative bone in your body. You should go work as a janitor and spare us your stupidity. Get out!"

Shocked, Marcello gathered his belongings and left the office. He was even more stunned when, the next afternoon, Cynthia phoned Marcello to find out why he had not come in to work. From Marcello's point of view, he had been publicly and unequivocally fired. Cynthia insisted that she did not fire Marcello but, rather, had just been blowing off some steam after a stressful week, and that she had not meant anything by her comments.

DISCUSSION QUESTIONS

1. Was Marcello's employment terminated? Why do you think he was or was not terminated?

2. Did Cynthia's behaviour affect the working relationship between her and Marcello, or between Marcello and his other colleagues?

3. Would this incident constitute as constructive dismissal?

4. How would you advise Cynthia's boss in this instance?

5. What coaching or other feedback would you have for Cynthia?

6. Would you bring Marcello back to work? What would be required to have him return to the office given this incident?

SCENARIO 2

Marcello has worked as a graphic designer in a small boutique ad agency for the past two years. There was always pressure to meet deadlines, and working with a creative, driven group was often stressful. Still, he loved his job, despite the many flare-ups in the office.

However, lately Marcello's boss, Cynthia, had been pretty hard on the team of eight. Their current client was unhappy with the ideas that the team had presented and they were in danger of losing the account. After a particularly heated pitch meeting in which Cynthia was criticizing the work of the team, Marcello stood up and yelled, "That's it! I'm sick of your criticism and bullying! You think you can yell at us all day and get away with it. Well, you can't! I quit!" Marcello stormed out of the meeting and left the building.

The next day Marcello came to work as if nothing had happened. While he looked a little withdrawn, he did not speak to anyone about the incident in the meeting. Cynthia was confused: from her perspective, Marcello had unequivocally quit his job. From Marcello's perspective, he had just lost his cool during a heated meeting and had expressed his frustrations, but did not really intend to quit.

Cynthia has asked to speak to you as she is unsure of how to handle this situation.

DISCUSSION QUESTIONS

1. Did Marcello quit?

2. What criteria needs to be considered in order to have a resignation?

3. What are the contextual circumstances that have to be considered in this scenario that might have an effect on the outcome?

4. How would you advise Cynthia in this instance?

5. How would you coach Marcello in this instance?

CASE STUDY 14

THE OFFICE ROMANCE

SCENARIO 1

It is Monday morning and you are catching up on your e-mail with a cup of coffee. The day started off quietly, but then you notice a message marked "Urgent!" from Bob Nuance, manager of the sales department in your company, Jesse Holdings. The e-mail said,

> Good morning. I need to talk to you about Joanie and Vassily. People are starting to get upset in the department. While it is no secret that Joanie and Vassily are involved, others on the team are complaining to me about their "public displays of affection" and how they keep making "googly eyes" at one another during meetings and throughout the day. It's distracting to everyone and no one is making any sales these days!

Joanie Bell is an Account Manager who has worked for the company for three years. She is a good employee and her clients like her. Last year, she won an achievement award from the company for being one of the top three grossing salespeople. This year so far, she has not done as well, and you wonder if her new office romance with Vassily is distracting her.

Vassily Petrov has been with the company for seven years and is also considered a top salesperson, although, he has not been in the top three for some years. You recall that, two years ago, Vassily went through a hostile divorce that affected him both personally and professionally. He and Joanie started dating seven months ago, and Vassily has seemed younger and happier these days.

Joanie and Vassily have not kept their budding romance a secret, but you are concerned about the morale on the team these days, as you have been hearing grumblings about the relationship. Your company does not have a policy about office romances, and there have been other instances in the past of coworkers dating each other. In fact, at least two couples met and married while working for Jesse Holdings in recent years.

DISCUSSION QUESTIONS

1. How would you approach this situation?

2. What advice would you give to Bob Nuance?

3. What discussions, if any, would you have with Joanie and Vassily? Would you speak with them individually or together?

4. Would you address this situation with the sales team? If yes, how?

5. Should Jesse Holdings draft a formal policy on office romances? Research to find examples of similar office romance policies. Would you recommend implementing one?

SCENARIO 2

It is Monday morning and you are catching up on your e-mail with a cup of coffee. The day started off quietly, but then you notice a message marked "Urgent!" from Bob Nuance, manager of the sales department in your company, Jesse Holdings. The e-mail said,

> Good morning. I need to talk to you. People are starting to get upset in the department because of the rumours about Joanie and Vassily. It's distracting to everyone and no one is making any sales these days!

Joanie Bell is an Account Manager who has worked for the company for three years. She is a good employee and her clients like her. Last year, she won an achievement award from the company for being one of the top three grossing salespeople, although this year she has not done as well.

Vassily Petrov has been with the company for seven years and is also considered a top salesperson, although he has not been in the top three for some years.

Joanie and Vassily are both married to other people. Rumours of an affair between them started about four months ago, but you have been unable to confirm it. One of their coworkers, Eden, a devout Christian, had complained to you about what she believes is "immoral behaviour." At the time, you told her – politely, of course – to mind her own business and not to engage in office gossip. But you can see from Bob's e-mail that the situation may be getting worse.

DISCUSSION QUESTIONS

1. How would you approach this situation?

2. What advice would you give to Bob Nuance?

3. What discussions, if any, would you have with Joanie and Vassily? Would you speak with them individually or together?

4. Would you address Eden again? If so, what would you say?

5. Does the fact that Joanie and Vassily are both married make a difference to your approach? Would you have the same concerns if they were both single?

6. Should Jesse Holdings draft a formal policy on office romances? Research to find examples of similar office romance policies. Would you recommend implementing one?

7. What recommendation would you make in this scenario?

SCENARIO 3

It is Monday morning and you are catching up on your e-mail with a cup of coffee. The day started off quiet, but then you notice a message marked "Urgent!" from Bob Nuance, director of the sales department in your company, Jesse Holdings. The e-mail said,

> Good morning. I need to talk to you. People are starting to get upset in the department because of the rumours about Joanie and Vassily. It's distracting to everyone and no one is making any sales these days!"

Joanie Bell is an Account Manager who has worked for the company for three years. She is a good employee and her clients like her. Last year, she won an achievement award from the company for being one of the top three grossing salespeople, although this year she has not done as well.

Vassily Petrov oversees the sales department and is Joanie's direct manager. He has been with the company for seven years and was promoted due to his strengths as a top salesperson and a charismatic leader. Clients love him, as do most of his staff.

Joanie and Vassily are both single. Rumours of an affair between them started about four months ago, but you have been unable to confirm it. Other team members have been complaining about favouritism, believing that Joanie is getting preferential treatment due to their relationship. From Bob's e-mail, you can see that the situation may be getting worse.

DISCUSSION QUESTIONS

1. How would you approach this situation?

2. What advice would you give to Bob Nuance?

3. What discussions, if any, would you have with Joanie and Vassily? Would you speak with them individually or together?

4. Does the fact that Joanie reports to Vassily make a difference to your approach? Would you have the same concerns if they were peers instead?

5. What recommendation would you make in this scenario?

CASE STUDY 15

THE TRAINEE

SCENARIO 1

Fleur Airlines hires over fifty people per month into their eight-week Call Centre Agents training program. The training program is intensive and competitive; however, the company receives many applicants, primarily because of the company perk of free travel for all employees anywhere the airline flies.

In this program, participants are required to write and pass an exam every Friday; trainees scoring below 85% on the exam are permitted one opportunity to re-write it and, if they score below 85% a second time, they are terminated from the program and their employment is ended. Typically, out of the fifty new hires into the program, less than half complete the eight-week training and go on to have careers with the airline. Graduates of the program are considered elite employees due to the rigour of the training, and are often referred to as "Fleur-azons."

Cody Baskins has been in the program for two weeks. Prior to joining Fleur Airlines, he worked as a Marketing Representative for a promotional items company, Cosmo Marketing. At Cosmo, Cody was the second-highest commission earner due to his extraverted and aggressive style, but he wanted to try a career in the travel industry and so left Cosmo to join Fleur.

In his first two weeks, Cody proved to be a keen and vocal trainee. He asked a lot of questions and spoke up frequently. At first, his session trainer, Barbara Jablonsky, welcomed and encouraged Cody's enthusiasm. However, by the fourth day of the first week, Barbara noted that Cody's frequent questions interrupted the flow of the training and irritated the

other participants. More than once, she noticed the other trainees roll their eyes whenever Cody raised his hand to speak.

On the Friday of the second week, Barbara pulled Cody aside and said, "Cody, I appreciate your eagerness for the class, but I am asking if you could refrain from commenting so frequently. I would like to give equal time to the other participants to jump in with their questions as well." Cody agreed and said he would "tone it down from now on."

However, on the Monday of the third week, Cody called the Human Resources department and said that he wanted to lodge a complaint about Barbara. When you spoke with Cody, he told you that he believed Barbara was "out to get him" and that she was planning to fail him so that he would be terminated. He said that Barbara had singled him out and that he did not trust her as his trainer any longer.

DISCUSSION QUESTIONS

1. How would you approach this situation?

2. What questions would you ask Cody as part of his statement?

3. What questions would you ask Barbara as part of the investigation?

4. Would you question any other members of the training class?

5. What are the contextual circumstances that have to be considered in this scenario that might have an effect on the outcome?

6. Given that Cody has only been with Fleur Airlines for two weeks and that graduation from the program is not guaranteed, what advice would you give to Cody's and Barbara's manager?

SCENARIO 2

Fleur Airlines hires over fifty people per month into their eight-week Call Centre Agents training program. The training program is intensive and competitive; however, the company receives many applicants, primarily because of the company perk of free travel for all employees anywhere the airline flies.

In this program, participants are required to write and pass an exam every Friday; trainees scoring below 85% on the exam are permitted one opportunity to re-write it and, if they score below 85% a second time, they are terminated from the program and their employment is ended. Typically, out of the fifty new hires into the program, less than half complete the eight-week training and go on to have careers with the airline. Graduates of the program are considered elite employees due to the rigour of the training, and are often referred to as "Fleur-azons."

Cody Baskins has been in the program for two weeks. Prior to joining Fleur Airlines, he worked as a Marketing Representative for a promotional items company, Cosmo Marketing. At Cosmo, Cody was the second-highest commission earner due to his extraverted and aggressive style, but he wanted to try a career in the travel industry and so left Cosmo to join Fleur.

In his first two weeks, Cody proved to be a keen and vocal trainee. He asked a lot of questions and spoke up frequently. At first, his session trainer, Barbara Jablonsky, welcomed and encouraged Cody's enthusiasm. However, by the fourth day of the first week, Barbara noted that Cody's frequent questions interrupted the flow of the training and irritated the

other participants. More than once, she noticed the other trainees roll their eyes whenever Cody raised his hand to speak.

By the middle of the second week, Barbara had had enough. Addressing him in front of the other participants, she said, "Cody, could you please be quiet? Your interruptions are distracting the entire class!" Cody was surprised at Barbara's outburst and remained quiet for the rest of the day.

The next morning, Cody called the Human Resources department and said that he wanted to lodge a complaint about Barbara. He outlined the situation and said that Barbara had humiliated and embarrassed him in front of his peers. He told you that he wants Barbara fired for being a bully.

DISCUSSION QUESTIONS

1. How would you approach this situation?

2. What questions would you ask Cody as part of his statement?

3. What questions would you ask Barbara as part of the investigation?

4. Would you question any other members of the training class?

5. What are the contextual circumstances that have to be considered in this scenario that might have an effect on the outcome?

6. Do you propose a different approach and outcome in Scenario 2 compared with Scenario 1? Why or why not?

SCENARIO 3

Fleur Airlines hires over fifty people per month into their eight-week Call Centre Agents training program. The training program is intensive and competitive; however, the company receives many applicants, primarily because of the company perk of free travel for all employees anywhere the airline flies.

In this program, participants are required to write and pass an exam every Friday; trainees scoring below 85% on the exam are permitted one opportunity to re-write it and, if they score below 85% a second time, they are terminated from the program and their employment is ended. Typically, out of the fifty new hires into the program, less than half complete the eight-week training and go on to have careers with the airline. Graduates of the program are considered elite employees due to the rigour of the training, and are often referred to as "Fleur-azons."

Cody Baskins has been in the program for two weeks. Prior to joining Fleur Airlines, he worked as a Marketing Representative for a promotional items company, Cosmo Marketing. At Cosmo, Cody was the second-highest commission earner due to his extraverted and aggressive style, but he wanted to try a career in the travel industry and so left Cosmo to join Fleur.

In his first two weeks, Cody proved to be a keen and vocal trainee. He asked a lot of questions and spoke up frequently. At first, his session trainer, Barbara Jablonsky, welcomed and encouraged Cody's enthusiasm. However, by the fourth day of the first week, Barbara noted that Cody's frequent questions interrupted the flow of the training and irritated the

other participants. More than once, she noticed the other trainees roll their eyes whenever Cody raised his hand to speak.

At the end of the first week, Cody scored 86% on his exam. At the end of the second week, Cody scored 83% on his exam. After re-writing the exam, he scored 84%. Cody was terminated from the program.

However, on the following Monday, Cody called the Human Resources department and said that he wanted to lodge a complaint about Barbara. When you spoke with Cody, he told you that he believed Barbara had been "out to get him" and that she had planned to fail him so that he would be terminated. He said that Barbara had singled him out and bullied him during the class. He wanted to appeal his termination and said he would get a lawyer if he did not stay in the program.

DISCUSSION QUESTIONS

1. How would you approach this situation?

2. What questions would you ask Cody as part of his statement?

3. What questions would you ask Barbara as part of the investigation?

4. Would you question any other members of the training class?

5. What are the contextual circumstances that have to be considered in this scenario that might have an effect on the outcome?

6. Given that the program outline clearly stated the requirements for remaining in the program, would you allow Cody to appeal his termination?

RESOURCES

Legislation and case law change frequently and so, while resources are listed here, it is important to research and reference the most up-to-date information available for your jurisdiction when addressing employee relations issues.

Here are a few of the more common resources you would reference:

CANADA

- Canada Labour Code
- Canadian Human Rights Act
- Newfoundland and Labrador Labour Standards Act
- Newfoundland and Labrador Human Rights Act
- Prince Edward Island Employment Standards Act
- Prince Edward Island Human Rights Act
- Nova Scotia Labour Standards Code
- Nova Scotia Human Rights Act
- New Brunswick Employment Standards Act
- New Brunswick Human Rights Act

- Quebec Labour Standards

- Quebec Charter of Human Rights and Freedoms

- Ontario Employment Standards

- Ontario Human Rights Code

- Manitoba Employment Standards Code

- Manitoba Human Rights Code

- Saskatchewan Employment Act

- Saskatchewan Human Rights Code

- Alberta Employment Standards Code

- Alberta Human Rights Act

- British Columbia Employment Standards Act

- British Columbia Human Rights Code

- Nunavut Labour Standards Act

- Nunavut Human Rights Act

- Yukon Employment Standards Act

- Yukon Human Rights Act

- Northwest Territories Employment Standards Act

- Northwest Territories Human Rights Act

UNITED STATES OF AMERICA

- Fair Standards Labor Act (FSLA)
- Civil Rights Act of 1964

MEXICO

- Federal Labor Law (*Ley Federal del Trabajo*)

EUROPEAN UNION

- European Commission Labour Laws

INTERNATIONAL LABOUR ORGANIZATION (ILO)

- This United Nations agency brings together governments, employers and workers representatives of one hundred and eighty-seven member States, to set labour standards, develop policies and devise programs promoting decent work for all women and men. You can find information on labour laws, standards, policies, and statistics by country on their web site.

ACKNOWLEDGEMENTS

Anyone who thinks that Human Resources is boring or transactional clearly is not paying attention. The cases featured in this book are just a sampling of the daily issues that a Human Resources professional deals with. Although they are a fictional depiction of employee relations situations, they are representative of the challenges that arise when dealing with different circumstances, different contexts, or even different cultures and laws.

My thanks to my editor Sheryl Khanna for guiding me through this process and for giving me advice on how to publish a book, and to Dr. Laura Hambley, who very generously shared her knowledge and contacts with me so that this book can come to life.

I would also like to thank my colleagues Darin Markwart, Erick Phillips, Candice Herlihy, and Carla Meadows, who never cease to amaze me with their technical expertise and logic, and who inspired some of the cases in this book.

Many thanks to my early readers of this book, Mary Castorina and Helen Niforos, who gave me feedback on content and format and who encouraged me to write, write, write, and write some more.

Finally, but not least, my deepest gratitude for the support from Sophia Champ, who came up with several of the names and scenarios found in this book, and from Tom Champ, who believed I could and should do this.